MARKET ECONOMY

AND

THE STATE

GERMINAL G. VAN

MARKET ECONOMY
AND
THE STATE

Essays On Political Economy

Copyright©2019 by Germinal G. Van
All Rights Reserved
Book written by Germinal G. Van
Cover designed by Germinal G. Van
Published by Germinal G. Van and Kindle Direct Publishing
authorgerminalgvan@gmail.com
ISBN: 978-107-902-9239

Printed in the United States

By the Same Author

American Political Culture

Equal Under The Law

Essays On Issues (Volume 1)

Reflection On Identity Politics

The Efficiency of Capitalism

Democratic Socialism On Trial

The Problem of Egalitarianism

Income Inequality and Economics

Table of Contents

Introduction

Market Economy and the State is a collection of political essays focusing on political economy. These essays are independent from one another but treat the same subject: How government intervention complicates the process of economic mechanisms that we supposed to follow their course if there was no intervention. A set of these essays were published by the Libertarian Institute, Foundation for Economic Education and the Mises Institute. The other set of these essays was unpublished. This book contains thirteen short-essays in politics, and economics.

The purpose of compiling these essays together to make it a book, was to give to the reader a broader approach about political economy for anyone who has no basic knowledge in the field. Political economy is not necessarily economics per se. Economics is a social science that assesses human behavior in relation to economic mechanisms. It is the study of production, distribution, and consumption of goods and services. Political economy, on the other hand, is a branch of the field of economics. It is a field of study that evaluates how the economic mechanisms and the political process intertwine. Political economy principally deals with the study of the conditions under which production or consumption with limited parameters was organized in a nation-state. Political economy treats of economic questions at macro level of economic policy implementation. In this book, the essays written evaluate the relationship between the political process and the economic mechanism of the United States from an Austrian standpoint. By using the word "Austrian" I do not mean the demonym of the country of Austria. "Austrian" in this book is used to assert the philosophy of the Austrian School of Economics, in which it asseverates that economic and social activities provide greater output when the political process does not play a significant role in these activities. In fact, each of these essays argue for a non-intervention of the government in the economy. The reason for that is because, the state; has the third-party; disrupts the natural process of economic activities once it seeks to do good. It invigorates regulations that do not benefit the main actors of the economy but only those who enforce these rules. Each of these essays advocate for a total laissez-faire capitalism and a free-market economy.

1

Keynesian Economics Is doomed To Fail

Our country was initially founded on the principles of limited government, individual rights, and personal responsibility. These principles, obviously, were meant to give more economic freedom to the individual to undertake, to create, to stimulate and to innovate. However, since the Great Depression, this vision of personal responsibility, autonomy, and individual sovereignty, has drastically changed. It has primarily changed economically with the economic theory of British economist John Maynard Keynes.

John Maynard Keynes argued that the best way to stimulate economic growth is by letting government injecting more money in the economy at lower interest rates so that the masses could borrow more and spend more.[1] And the very purpose of this economic approach is strictly to stimulate demand in order to create supply. In other words, total demand by spending creates supply. It does sound good because the government puts more money in the hands of consumers. Who would not want to spend more? This approach to economics, although it may seem rational at first glance; is nonetheless unsustainable for two essential reasons.

---

[1] Chappellow, Jim, "Keynesian Economics" *Investopedia,* (2019).

The first reason is that it produces short-term gains. Indeed, during an economic recession, the government injects a significant quantity of money into circulation in order to stimulate the economy. It is called economic stimulus. However, printing an excessive quantity of money inflates the price of goods and services as well as it raises the rate of unemployment in the long run. Keynesian economics does create unemployment. It creates employment on a short-term basis and unemployment on a long-term basis by allowing the government to impose regulations on businesses, which eventually decrease the demand for labor and increase the labor cost.[2] The increase in labor cost makes it harder for private businesses to afford labor demands, and that difficulty in supplying labor

[2] Worstall, Tim, "If You're A Keynesian Then You Must Believe The Minimum Wage Increases Unemployment" *Forbes*, (2015). Article. Web.

increases unemployment rate.[3] For example, unemployment rate under FDR was in the double-digit, precisely at 14 percent after his economic stimulus was implemented.[4] During the first eight years of his presidency, however, unemployment rate was at 18 percent before being brought down to 14 percent.[5] The point is that, when unemployment is in the double-digit, it means that the labor market is not doing great. In fact, we should be alarmed when unemployment is at 10 percent and above because the natural rate of unemployment is between 4.5 and 5 percent.[6] FDR though was the first American president to use Keynesian economic theory to deal with the Great Depression. FDR may

---

[3] Amadeo, Kimberly, "Seven Causes of Unemployment" *The Balance,* (2019). Article. Web.

[4] Moore, Stephen, "The Enduring Myth of FDR and the New Deal" *The Heritage Foundation.* (2014). Article. Web.

[5] Ibid.

[6] Amadeo, Kimberly, "Natural Rate of Unemployment, Its Components, and Recent Trends" *The Balance,* (2019). Article. Web.

have stabilized the economy in the late 30s and early 40s, but the galloping rate of unemployment and the augmentation of inflation rate in the 40s and 50s show that his economic policies were of short-term benefits and generated more unemployment in the long-run.[7]

The second reason for the unsustainability of Keynesian economic theory is that it merely amplifies the power of government over economic affairs. The problem with government intervention is that it enables bureaucrats to literally manage the means of production of an industry. By letting government having the power to control the quantity of money supply as well as the business cycle through regulations, Keynesian economic theory basically legitimizes central-planning

---

[7] "Inflation and CPI Consumer Price Index 1940-1949" *Inflation Data.* (2019). Data.

economics on the one hand and constrains the freedom of individuals to make their own economic decisions on the other hand. When government is in charge of managing the resources of an industry, it ends up mismanaging these resources because it reduces the prices of goods and services within that industry below its natural level, and delivers a poor quality of service to the consumers.[8] Innovation becomes stagnant and prices continue to rise in the long run because of inflation, although the productivity of that industry becomes motionless. A perfect example is Medicare and Medicaid. These two government-mandated programs are the downside of our national healthcare system. Prices of medical products and services under these two programs are expensive and their quality of service

---

[8] Scott Morton, Fiona M. "The Problems of Price Controls" *Cato Institute.* (2001). Article. Web.

continues to deteriorate[9] because their coverage only offers the bare minimum, which is, of course, not enough to solve the medical issues of each person.

Keynesian economics is an unsustainable economic theory that only makes government more powerful than it should be. But western governments still using it despite the fact that it has been proven to be a long-term deficient policy. Why western governments still use it then? Simply because it makes bureaucrats more powerful and gives them more leverage.[10] Keynesian economics is doomed to fail regardless of the circumstances. Government spends the money it does not have and ends up borrowing more than it needs. This excess of money borrowing creates inflation and that

---

[9] Ibid.
[10] Garrison, Roger, W. "The Absurdity of Keynesian Economics." *Mises Institute.* (2018). Article. Web.

inflation makes the economy stagnant. It is objectively fair to say that Keynesian economics slows economic productivity on a long-term basis.

2

Mixed Economy and the Danger of Central-Planning

In 1944, Friedrich von Hayek, one of the greatest economists and political philosophers in modern history; published his magnum opus entitled *The Road to Serfdom*. In his book, Hayek warned free societies about the dangers of government intervention. He argued that government intervention leads to totalitarianism. The Great Depression and World War II were the two main factors that encouraged most first-world countries to embrace government intervention and central-planning to solve problems. Today, most countries in the world, and especially developed nations, including the United States; have adopted a mixed economy in which the free-market policies and socialist policies must coexist in order to advance the common good.

Many intellectuals argue that a mixed economy is a better economic system than a laissez-faire economy or a command economy because it alleviates economic and social inequalities between social classes. For example, the policy of affordable housing, which enables those at the bottom of the social hierarchy to find housing; is a concrete result of a mixed economy in which the government plays a substantial role in social affairs, although the market economy continues to be promulgated by private initiatives. Notwithstanding, the main predicament of a mixed economy is that government intervention in economic and social affairs amplifies its authority over the lives of the citizens. The more the power of government expands, the more individual liberties are reduced. The minimum wage law is a perfect illustration of government control over the economy as Hayek has predicted. On the social aspect, the minimum wage law seems legitimate because it allows the worker to receive an adequate pay for the production of his labor. The wage he earns cannot be below the level of subsistence. On the economic aspect though, the minimum wage law is essentially a deficient factor of a mixed economy. Indeed, the implementation of the minimum wage law is a problem in the market economy because it penalizes low-skilled individuals to find employment and it, therefore, impedes the utility of human capital. The minimum wage law compels the employer to discriminate against low-skilled individuals and also forces the employer to increase the price of his products or services in order to remain competitive on the market. Each time the government increases the minimum wage, the employer or business owner is obliged to reduce his workforce in order to maintain his business. According to an article on *Inc.com,* which is titled *"Small Businesses Will Be Strangled by a $15 Minimum Wage,"* raising the minimum wage to $15 an hour has already begun to adversely affect small business at the local level. The City Council of Seattle raised its local minimum wage from $9.47 to $13 in 2016 with the goal of eventually making it $15 by 2021.[11] Mayor Murray insisted that Seattle's economy is thriving, employers are competing for workers, and workers who perform low-wage jobs,

---

[11] Arora, Rohit, *Small Businesses Will Be Strangled By a $15 Minimum Wage,* Inc.com. (2017). Article. Web.

such as dishwashing or food delivery, start at $15 or $20 per hour.[12] A study by economists at the University of Washington says it otherwise. Their study found that low wage workers' incomes actually fell by an estimated $125 a month because employers reduced their hours.[13] Raising the wage to $13 an hour yielded an average 3 percent in wages.[14] However, employers cut workers' hours by 9 percent.[15] It subsequently becomes a waste of human capital. If the government did not impose a minimum wage law, many low-skilled individuals would find employment whereas it is part-time or even temporarily; which would enable them to meet end needs.

---

[12] *Ibid.*

[13] *Ibid.*

[14] *Ibid.*

[15] *Ibid.*

A mixed economy is actually the steppingstone that leads to central-planning. And this is the real danger for classical liberalism because it subverts individual freedoms, and the free exchange of good and services between individuals and businesses. The reason a mixed economy is pernicious to the development of the free-market is because the government has redundant powers over public affairs. This implies that the government is actually used as the great equalizer whom alone has the power and authority to uphold economic and social equality through compulsive and coercive methods such as the progressive income taxation, and the creation of social programs like Food Stamps, TANF or Medicare and Medicaid. The only way for the state to maintain its role as the great equalizer, is by the enforcement of central economic planning, wherein the government has control over the mechanism of economic and social operations. Central-planning is an inherently defective and an unsustainable system. Ludwig von Mises is his book entitled *Socialism: An Economic and Sociological Analysis* published in 1922, demonstrated that central-planning is rationally impossible to adequately work. He explicitly stated that:

"The fundamental objection advanced against the practicability of socialism refers to the impossibility of economic calculation. It has been demonstrated in an irrefutable way that a socialist commonwealth would not be in a position to apply economic market prices for factors of production because they are neither bought nor sold, it is impossible to resort to calculation in planning future action and in determining the result of past action. A socialist management of production would simply not know whether or not what it plans and executes is the most appropriate means to attain the ends sought. It will operate in the dark,

as it were. It will squander the scarce factors of production both material and human (labour). Chaos and poverty for all will unavoidably results."[16]

This powerful quote of Ludwig von Mises extracted from *Socialism* can be clearly exemplified with the current situation of socialized medicine in the United Kingdom where its healthcare system is completely under central-planning of the British government. The National Health Services (NHS), which is the government agency that regulates and controls medicine in the United Kingdom. The NHS has proved to be a detrimental and flawed program for the British healthcare system for two main reasons. The first reason is that, although more people have access to the healthcare in the UK, they

---

[16] Ludwig von Mises, "Ludwig von Mises on the Impossibility of Rational Economic Planning Under Socialism (1922)", *Online Library of Liberty*, Quotation.

do not have the freedom to choose the medical plan that would fit their needs, nor the doctor of their choice. They are forced to go along with the medical plan that the government offers them, which is a plan with limited options. The government imposes on the patients what it believes is best for them without knowing their needs nor the signals that would stimulate innovation in the medical industry. The second reason is the mismanagement of the central-planning in the medical industry. The government controls the prices of drugs and the cost of medical treatments. Although patients pay nothing when they are receiving treatments, the British government yearly increases taxes so it could maintain its medical supply. But the problem is that government increases taxes, but the medical supply is still of low-quality. Through the 1960s and 1970s, the NHS has begun to malfunction. Demand exceeded supply, and the system faced a shortage of doctors, nurses, and medical treatments because the government failed to maintain the equilibrium necessary to sustain the stimulus. The National Institute for Health and Care Excellence (NICE) is responsible for approving new drugs and treatments for the NHS.[17] The drug infliximab for example, is used to treat ulcerative colitis, but it was not prescribed for those with Crohn's disease—why? Because there are more Crohn's patients and the treatments would cost more.[18] Even when treatments are available for some conditions, the NHS often does not act in the best interests of patients.[19] The NHS was built on the mantra that

---

[17] Allison, Andrew, "The NHS's Flaws Are Killing Us", *Comment Central,* (2018. Article. Web.

[18] *Ibid.*

[19] *Ibid.*

treatment is available to all, free at the point of use, regardless of the patient's ability to pay.[20] What the NHS does not publicize is that the best treatments available to patients in other countries are not necessarily available in the United Kingdom.[21] If the healthcare system was privatized, the medical industry would have thrived three times faster than the current one. It would have thrived faster because individuals would have brought innovation since they have the knowledge through prices, production, and capital; of what is necessary to foster the betterment of the healthcare system.

Mixed economies are fallacious because they are explicitly mixed. On the contrary, they are progressively moving towards more government

---

[20] *Ibid.*

[21] *Ibid.*

intervention, therefore, towards more central planning; that is to say towards absolute control of the state over economic and social affairs. It is important and even wise that the authority of the state be substantially reduced in economic and social affairs so that individuals can prosper without interventionist and coercive force.

Essay published on the Libertarian Institute on May 15, 2019

3

The Three Myths of the Minimum Wage

The 2020 presidential election is rapidly approaching with key issues discussed between political candidates and voters. One issue that has been reiterated is the potential increase of the national minimum wage. The federal minimum wage is today set at $7.25 an hour since 2009. Many prominent presidential hopefuls in the Democratic Party such as Bernie Sanders, Elizabeth Warren, Cory Booker, Kamala Harris, Tulsi Gabbard, Robert Francis O'Rourke, Peter Buttigieg and Julian Castro; have all advocated for increasing the minimum wage to $15 an hour on the premise that surging the minimum wage to $15 an hour would help low-skilled workers make living wage and would benefit the economy as a whole.

For too long, the American people have always believed that increasing the minimum wage would benefit the economy as well as it would improve their living standard. But this long-standing statement is a myth that contains three misleading presumptions. The first premise is that; augmenting the minimum wage helps businesses thriving. The second premise is that increasing the minimum wage would facilitate the obtainment of employment for low-skilled workers. The third and most important premise is that surging the minimum wage helps attaining living wage. These three assertions need to be tested with empirical evidence in order to determine their truthfulness on the matter.

First Myth: Increasing the minimum wage helps businesses to thrive

The first premise avows that augmenting the minimum wage helps businesses thriving. Many cities have minimum wages that go beyond their state's minimum wage such as Seattle, or San Francisco, that require businesses to gradually raise their minimum wages to $15 an hour.[22] Overall 21 states and Washington, D.C.[23] have raised their minimum wage to the $15-per-hour-track. Augmenting the minimum wage may be beneficial to big businesses and corporations such as Walmart or Amazon because they worth billions of dollars.

---

[22] Gardner, Karen, "The Effects of Minimum Wage on Business" *Chron.* (2019). Article. Web.
[23] Ibid.

However, the augmentation of the minimum wage does not help businesses, especially small and mid-size businesses, thriving for the mere reason that these businesses are compelled to increase the price of their products and services in order to stay in business and compete otherwise they will have to shorten their staff or go bankrupt. The incrementation of the price of goods and services suggests that the labor cost is also going to increase. A recent study from Harvard Business School investigates how minimum wage affected the restaurant industry.[24] The study shows for example that a $1 increase in the minimum wage leads to a 14 percent increase in the likelihood of exit for the median 3.5 median star restaurant, although it may

---

[24] Dara Lee Luca and Michael Luca, "Survival of the Fittest: The Impact of the Minimum Wage on Firm Exit" *Harvard Business School.* (2017-2018). Study Data.

not necessarily hurt five-star restaurants.[25] According to the Small Business Administration, small businesses provide 55 percent of all jobs and 66 percent of all net new jobs since the 1970s in the United States.[26] Moreover, 28 million small businesses account for 54 percent of all U.S. sales.[27] These results show that small businesses play a substantial with the U.S. economy.[28] Increasing the minimum wage to $15 will adversely affect their growth.[29]

Second Myth: Increasing the minimum wage facilitates the obtainment of entry-level jobs for low-skilled workers

---

[25] Ibid.

[26] Cost-Benefits Analysis (CBA) *U.S. Small Business Administration.* Data.

[27] Ibid.

[28] Chabra Esha, "Small Businesses Struggling With $15 Minimum Wage, New Site Reports" *Forbes,* (2017). Article. Web.

[29] Ibid.

The second premise asserts that increasing the minimum wage will make it easier for low-skilled workers to obtain entry-level employment. In fact, the minimum wage was initially implemented to help low-skilled workers obtaining an entry-level position on the labor market. Despite the fact that the intent of the government was truly genuine, data show that increasing the minimum wage actually hurts those that it intended to help; that is to say, the low-skilled workers. There is one fundamental thing that escapes the knowledge of the average American regarding the minimum wage. Indeed, most Americans are unaware that whenever the minimum wage increases, the level of qualifications for obtaining an entry-level position also increases. Evidence from the Employment Policies Institute substantiates that the incrementation of the minimum wage hurts the availability of economic opportunities for low-skilled workers. As a matter of fact, entry-level positions often represent the only employment opportunity for those with limited education or high school dropouts.[30] Sixty years of economic research, including recent studies, have shown that low-wage, low-skilled employees are the most likely to lose their jobs after a mandated wage hike.[31] Only 1.8 percent of American workers earned the federal minimum wage or below in 2015. This is because employers have to offer above minimum wage pay to retain talented workers.[32] When employers are required to pay more, they choose workers with more skills and combine them with technology, such as digital ordering.[33] As a result,

---

[30] Flynn, Mike, "Minimum wage hikes hurt low-skilled workers" *Employment Policies Institute,* (2006). Article. Web.

[31] Ibid.

[32] Furchtgott-Roth, Diana, "Column: Raising the Minimum Wage Lowers Employment for Teens and Low-Skill Workers" *PBS News Hour.* (2016). Article. Web.

[33] Ibid.

low-skilled workers lose their jobs. Another evidence shows that increasing the minimum wage negatively affects low-skilled workers.[34] As a practical matter, a recent study demonstrated that the recent increases in the minimum wage were responsible for 14 percent of the decline in the share of the working-age population employed between 2006 and 2012.[35] The study founded that minimum wage increases significantly reduced the probability of low-skilled worked reaching the middle-class.[36] Every time the minimum wage increases, employers also increase the level of qualifications to obtain an entry-level job. As of today, since many areas in the United States have a minimum wage that is way

---

[34] Ibid.

[35] Jeffrey Clemens and Matthew Wither, "The Minimum Wage and the Great Recession: Evidence of Effects On the Employment and Income Trajectories of Low-Skilled Workers" *National Bureau of Economic Research*. (2014). Study-Data.

[36] Ibid.

above the federal minimum wage, most employers require prospective job applicants to have at least a college degree with some work experience; just to qualify for an entry-level position. It logically indicates then that if the minimum wage were to be increased to $15-an-hour, a job applicant ought to have a master's degree in order to obtain an entry-level job. In other words, increasing the minimum wage will simply cut entry-level jobs, therefore, more low-skilled workers would be unemployed.[37]

Third Myth: Increasing the minimum wage makes a living wage

The third premise is probably the most misleading and unsubstantiated assumption that encompasses all the myths regarding the minimum

---

[37] Ortiz, Alfredo, "Raising the Minimum Wage Will Cut Entry-Level Jobs" *Real Politics*, (2018). Article. Web.

wage. Senator Sanders, in particular, has reiterated that statement in each of his rallies that increasing the minimum wage would lead to a living wage. It is a very fallacious assumption because the living wage is not based on the minimum wage. The living wage is based on the market value and the market value is based on the rate of inflation. The average American must understand that the fundamental reason as of why bureaucrats in Washington and state governments increase the minimum wage every year, is simply because they need to keep up with inflation. As the market value is based on the inflation rate, when the prices of goods and services inflate, the living standard also inflates because an equilibrium needs to be maintained otherwise an economic bust will occur. If the living standard of a given area increases, the purchasing power of the consumer in that area, on the other hand, decreases because the latter will not have enough money to spend. Increasing the minimum wage concurrently surges the living wage and diminishes the purchasing power of the consumer. Consumers would have less to spend if prices are high because they cannot afford it. Therefore, demand will plummet. A 2016 poll conducted by the Pew Research Center indicates that 58 percent of the American people are in favor of increasing the minimum wage to $15 an hour.[38] They support this boost without fully comprehend the economic impact behind that boost. It is preponderant to grasp that the living wage is not a standardized component. It fluctuates according to the market value. Consequently, the real value of a $15 minimum wage would depend on where each of us

---

[38] Minimum Wage" *Pew Research Center* (2016). Data.

lives.[39] Living costs not only vary throughout the country, but they can also vary within individual states as well.[40] Giving low-paid workers everywhere in the country the same real purchasing power would require hundreds of different minimum wages, scaled to each locality cost of living.[41] For example, a low-skilled worker paid at $13 an hour in Waco, Texas can afford a living wage because the living wage is lower since the market value in Waco is lower.[42] If that same low-skilled worker were paid $13 or $14 and lived in Washington, D.C.; that worker would be in the poverty threshold because the minimum wage in Washington, D.C. is $14 an hour and the market value there is significantly

---

[39] DeSilver, Drew, "The Real Value of a $15 minimum wage depends on where you live" *Pew Research Center*. (2018). Article. Web.

[40] Ibid.

[41] Ibid.

[42] "Living Wage Calculator for Waco, Texas." *Living Wage Calculator*, (2019). Data.

higher.[43] It suggests that a low-skilled worker living in places like Washington, D.C., San Francisco or New York City, has a higher likelihood to remain poor than if he was living in Kentucky, Texas, or Georgia.

Regardless of where we stand whether it is politically or ideologically, we shall recognize that the minimum wage, despite its noble intentions, is not the salvation that the American people have expected from it. Raising the minimum wage will not make everyone better-off overall. Too many different factors are involved in the process to determine if increasing the minimum wage nationally is a good idea. Nonetheless, empirical evidence has already demonstrated the effect it

---

[43] Living Wage Calculator for District of Columbia," *Living Wage Calculator*. (2019). Data.

would have on businesses, and individuals if it were to be surged.

4

The Role of Government Is Not to Stimulate The Economy But to Let It Regulate Itself

It is undeniable that the majority of the American people believe that the national economy is a top priority. Indeed, according to the Pew Research Center, 70 percent agree that the economy is among the highest priorities.[44] In 2011, following the Great Recession of 2008, 87 percent of the electorate called it a "top priority."[45] If the economy is, in fact,

---

[44] Editorials, "Public 2019 Priorities: Economy, Healthcare, Education and Security All Near Top of List," *Pew Research Center*, (2019). Article. Data.
[45] Ibid.

a priority, then how should its growth be maintained? As of today 71 percent of the American believe that the federal government should stimulate the economy.[46] It entails that over two-third of the American electorate agrees with the assumption that the federal government should regulate the economy. These numbers show that the American people rather rely on the government's lead instead of entrusting their own judgment to make economic decisions. It is important, however, to understand the reasons that have led the majority of the American people to believe that the government has the solutions to provide economic growth. As a matter of fact, Americans believe that economic stimulus prevents recession and reduce income inequality. Interestingly, none of these two

---

[46] Ibid.

beliefs have been proven valid because the evidence shows a result contrary to these premises.

President Reagan, who used to be called "the Great Communicator" due to his flawless communication skills, once famously said during his Inaugural Address in 1981: "Government is not the solution to our problem; government is the problem."[47] Today, it seems evidently clear that the American people have drastically veered from that principle of limited government promulgated by the 40th President of the United States.

Since the Great Depression, the American people are convinced that the government is the solution to solve an economic crisis. The major economic crisis that has occurred since the Great Depression was the Great Recession of 2008. The

---

[47] Rosenberg, Jennifer, "32 Ronald Reagan Quotes You Should Know" *ThoughtCo.* (2019). Article. Web.

Great Recession drove many Americans to lose their homes; unemployment skyrocketed from 5 percent in 2007 to 9.5 percent in June 2009 and surged to 10 percent in October 2009. The federal government has injected $700 billion into circulation to stimulate the economy.[48] The point of this economic stimulus was to increase the money supply in order to boost demand; and that demand in return would create supply. This Keynesian practice may work, but it only works on a short-term basis. What most Americans don't see is that, when the government becomes the arbitrator, the one that regulates economic activities, it controls prices, imposes regulations on businesses, and stock markets and reduces economic incentives. In addition to this problem, the political process itself can stunt

---

[48] "The Recession of 2007-2009" *Bureau of Labor Statistics.* (2012). Data.

economy. For example, Professor Emeritus of Law at George Mason University Gordon Tullock suggests that politicians and bureaucrats try to gain control of as much of the economy as possible.[49] Furthermore, demand for government resources by the private sector leads to misallocation of resources.[50] Proponents of government spending often point to the fiscal multiplier as a way that spending can fuel growth.[51] However, based on evidence provided by the National Bureau of Economic Research (NBER), government spending has a strong negative correlation with business investment.[52] Government spending reduces savings in the economy, thus increasing interest rates.[53] The

---

[49] Thomas Stratmann and Gabriel Lucjan Okolski, "Does Government Spending Affect Economic Growth?" *Mercatus Center George Mason University.* (2010). Study. Monetary Policy.
[50] Ibid.
[51] Ibid.
[52] Ibid.
[53] Ibid.

incrementation of interest rates disincentivizes businesses and individuals to borrow more money and make more investments that would increase their output.

Income inequality has been a substantial issue within the American social order. Politicians always talk about income inequality. They pretend to have the solution to attenuate the problem. And the American people continue to believe them as if these politicians would cure the issue. The government, through collected taxes, redistributes allocated funds to selected economic entities, not only through transfer of payments as well as the financing and provision of public goods and utilities such as education or health.[54] For example, the single-payer system proposed by Senator Sanders, if

---

[54] Madzinova, Renata, "The Impact of Government Spending on Income Inequality" *Department of Economics Management and Marketing, College Business, Duchnovičovo,* (2018). Study.

implemented, would be funded solely by the taxpayer in which a small group of people would have to be compelled to spend more than the two-third of the country on the premise that those who are wealthy should pay their "fair-share." Annual federal, state, and local government spending from all sources, including tax subsidies, now totals more than $60,000 per household.[55] We surely know that a $60,000-household is a middle-class family in America. The social bracket that the government uses the most to fund its programs is the middle-class. Bureaucrats argue to have the solution to narrow the income inequality gap. But solution blindsides the middle-class itself. That solution is to tax the middle-class the most than any other social class. Many flawed tax policies are rooted in the

---

[55] Steuerle, Eugene, "Prioritizing Opportunity for All In the Federal Budget" *Urban Institute*. (2016). Article. Web.

ability of affluent households to delay or even avoid tax on the returns from their wealth.[56] The Congressional Budget Office finds that the fifth of the population with the highest income saw their share rise from 46 to 55 percent between 1979 and 2014.[57] This increase in income inequality came about despite the growth in Social Security, Medicare, and Medicaid, which boot before-tax-income for low and middle-class households.[58]

Government stimulus may sound good theoretically, but practically, it only delivers short-term outcomes. People are better-off when the government plays a less intrusive role in the economy. We always complain about the costs of living, bills, the cost of healthcare, education, and

---

[56] Steuerle, Eugene, "How Government Tax and Transfer Policy Promotes Wealth Inequality" *Tax Policy Center,* (2019). Article. Study.
[57] Analysts, "How Do Taxes Affect Income Inequality?" *Tax Policy Center.* (2019). Data.
[58] Ibid.

other social industries. But the cost of all of these social industries that invigorate our economy is expensive because we let the government, which is the third-party, being in charge of prices and economic regulations. Economic growth works better when the people are in charge of their own business, they can determine prices, and expand human capital, and develop production without government interference. Individuals know best for themselves what the third-party would obviously not know. Government stimulus does not make our economy sustainable.

5

Government Regulations:
The Roots of Income Inequality

It is undeniable that any civil society needs regulations. And the best entity to enforce these regulations is the state. Therefore, a state is needed to ensure that society is properly conducted. John Locke, the Father of Classical Liberalism, made it clear in his magnum opus; *Second Treatise of Government;* that individuals living in a civil and politically organized society; do need a state for three main reasons. First and foremost, civilized people needed a state to protect the life of members of society, consequently, to protect each other from coercion. That is why the implementation of the police is quintessential for society to be ordered. Secondly, civilized people needed the state to protect the liberty of each member of society so that individuals can freely pursue their own self-interests. That is why it has never been the role of the government to intervene in the economic affairs of society; but instead, to let individuals pursue their own interests so long as they do not harm one another. Thirdly, civilized people needed the state to protect private property. Each member of society, by natural law, has to right to retain private property because private property can only be earned through the production of labour. That is why the courts exits; to enforce contracts among individuals and to protect private property. Of course, the state can only preserve these three fundamental negative rights through regulations, otherwise, it will be a complete anarchy. We can, subsequently, all agree that a state is needed to ensure the sustentation of these rights. Nonetheless, John Locke was very well wary of the potential excess of power a government could have if it retained too much authority. So, he argued that although it is the role of government to protect these undeniable and inalienable rights, which belong to the individual; the power of government must be limited in order for the state to not encroach the rights the individuals it is meant to protect. Now, the main interrogation remains on the role of the state. To what extent is the state needed in the life of the citizens?

Our constitution has clearly defined the powers of our government. We had a constitution that favors private ownership, and the pursuit of economic self-interests. However, through the evolution of the republic, the power of the central government has substantially aggrandized. The reason for this aggrandizement has been this myth regarding the resentment of capitalism and free-market. The Great Depression is, evidently, the turning point in American political history. It was taught to the younger generations that the Great Depression occurred because of a failure of the free-market, and that government regulations were necessary to restore the economy. It was since then that the government entered into economic affairs with the implementation of regulations over regulations. We have become dependent on the government to regulate the market and to redistribute the wealth.

The main issue with this is that government regulations have created more problems than providing solutions. One of the principal issues that government regulations have generated, is income inequality. Income inequality truly commenced when the government effectuated regulations such as the minimum wage law and regulations on businesses. Before the implementation of the minimum wage law, any individual; regardless of his skin color or religion; could be employed because employers were looking for people who will bring value to the job market. The absence of a minimum wage law enabled individuals to not only earn a salary but also to be lifted out of poverty. The enforcement of the minimum wage law since 1938 has simply made it harder for low-income individuals to obtain employment and live comfortably. The incrementation of the minimum wage also incremented the qualifications that an individual needed to be competitive on the labor market. The higher the minimum wage becomes, the smaller the job market also becomes; especially for people who do not meet the requirements to be eligible. So, these people can either go on welfare, or simply be expose to the societal dangers that can propel them to jail. People will be better-off if there were less economic regulations; if the government did not try to regulate the market; if the government left individuals pursuing their own self-interests.

Furthermore, government intervention in the economy also engendered an enormous economic disparity between businesses and corporations. Government regulations give an advantage to corporations over startups and mid-size businesses. Albeit we do have a mixed economy, government's economic regulations enable corporations to retain and maintain a monopoly on market venues, which makes it very difficult for small businesses to compete. Only corporations can afford the incrementation of the minimum wage. Every time that the minimum wage is augmented, prices of products and services also increase. It entails that for a small business to stay competitive in the market, it has to increase the price of its products and services in order to compensate its staff; otherwise, it will have to shut down. Corporations like Wal-Mart and the Big Four Techs companies (Apple, Google, Amazon, Facebook) have the monetary power to afford paying its employees when the minimum wage increases; reduce prices of their products and services which makes it very affordable for customers. Therefore, these companies can impose their rules to consolidate their monopoly on the market, which attenuate competition and slowly drives small businesses out of business. Corporations are powerful because they have lobby groups to influence political power so that the government will implement policies which favor their interests. If the government was not involved in the economy, it would have been more difficult for corporations to withhold the monopoly of the means of productions. Today, we do not live in a true capitalistic, free-market economy. Our economic model is unfortunately commanded by corporatism. Government regulations in the economy have made it more difficult for people to genuinely prosper economically. So long as the federal government will continue to pass regulations that would give a competitive advantage to corporations over small businesses; the income inequality gap will simply continue to enlarge itself to the point that a revolution may have to occur in order to change the course of events.

6

Big Government Doesn't Make The Economy Better; It Worsens It

There is a myth that has been portrayed and displayed for years in economics. That myth is that when the market fails, the government must step in to restore economic growth. This myth has, in fact, been the cornerstone of the justification for FDR's big government policies. It has been taught to the modern-day American citizen that the Great Depression was a failure of free-market and private businesses; which is, in reality, the greatest myth in American economics. What has not been taught to the modern-day American citizen, is that the Great Depression did occur because of a failure of government monetary policy. That monetary policy which engendered the crash of the stock market in 1929 was the Real Bills doctrine. The Real Bills doctrine suggested that the Federal Reserve would supply a surplus of credit to commercial banks during times of economic expansion. But the Real Bills failed to propose a policy to attenuate the crash of the stock market during economic recession. The lack of adequate solutions to save private businesses and commercial banks during the recession stimulated the justification for the federal government to intervene in the economy. Since then, the government has ensconced a permanent foothold in the American economy. It is this permanent foothold that Stephanie Kelton wants the government to maintain.

Stephanie Kelton, for those who are not familiar with her, is a professor of economics, and the economic policy advisor for Bernie Sanders. She is a staunch supporter of Keynesian economics. The big government and socialistic economic policies of Bernie Sanders were, in fact, instigated and promulgated by Stephanie Kelton. Dr. Kelton has argued that the federal government can fund and subsidize any program it wishes to implement because it cannot go bankrupt.[59] She furthered her stance by stressing that; since the federal government cannot go bankrupt, it can, therefore, print as much money as it pleases it to fund its programs.[60] According to Dr. Kelton, the federal government can indefinitely, and single-handedly

---

[59] Helfand, Zach, "The Economist Who Believes The Government Should Just Print More Money" *The New Yorker,* (2019). Article. Web.
[60] Youngberg, David, "Bernie's Senior Economic Advisor Sees No Problem in Printing Unlimited Money" *Foundation for Economic Education (FEE).* Article. Web.

subsidize any programs such the single-payer system, the free college-tuition, public housing, jobs-for-all (the government can provide jobs to every single American citizen) ...etc.[61] Even though, Dr. Kelton's economic assessments may sound good and fair; they are; nonetheless; flawed, unsustainable, and unrealistic.

Dr. Kelton's economic policy is based on an economic model of central-planning. This indicates that the government holds the monopoly of prices and the means of production. If our economy uses a central-planning model, the federal government will have to continuously raise taxes in order to subsidize its programs. The flaw with using a central-planning style to stimulate economic growth is that the government eventually runs out of

---

[61] Sorman, Guy, "Return of The Neo-Keynesians" *City Journal*. (2019). Article. Web.

resources and money. The economy of a country is never a permanently sustainable mechanism. Each economy in every society, in every country on earth; has its expansions and recessions. During times of economic recession, the government must deregulate the economy by letting private investors subsidizing market venues through innovation. It is always significant for the government to not intervene during recession times because the economy recovers on its own with a new product being released. The release of that product or service generates more opportunities in the market. The creation of new products and services; and the determination of the prices of these products and services, will enable the germination of employment growth. It is quintessentially imperative that the government exerts a market economy, so that it can incentivizes competitivity among private businesses, which will inevitably stimulate economic growth.

Dr. Kelton's argument regarding the fact that the government can indefinitely print more money even during economic recession; is authentically flawed because a surplus of printing money during a recession leads to hyperinflation. This has been the case in Zimbabwe, and it is currently the case in Venezuela. When the government prints more money during times of recession, the price of basic goods costs three times, four times, or sometimes a thousand times more than its standard price. If for example, the single-payer system was our national healthcare system; during recession times; the federal government would have to print more money to subsidize medical supplies. The price of these medical supplies would unavoidably increase, which will terminate the free-charge that was initially implemented at the dawn of the program. It entails that medical care would no longer be free because patient will have to pay so the government can keep supplying medical care. Although the government may have the authority to indefinitely print money; doing so will only stagnate the economy rather than stimulating it. Printing money may be indefinite, but economic resources are not permanent, nor perpetual unless they are ceaselessly innovated. Consequently, the economic policy of Dr. Kelton will only damage the American economy as whole if government retains control of prices and the means of production.

7

The Problem With Elizabeth Warren's Wealth Tax Plan

Elizabeth Warren is among the strongest contenders and Democratic hopefuls for the presidential election of 2020. During the fourth Democratic debate, on October 15th, 2019, the economic policy of Elizabeth Warren also known as the "Wealth Tax Plan" got close attention regarding how it could reduce income inequality in the United States.

The central argument about the wealth tax proposal of Senator Warren is that; through a progressive wealth tax system,[62] which means those with higher income will pay higher taxes; the wealthiest people in America will pay their "fair share" and that fair share will enable the equal redistribution of wealth. Set forth by French economists, Thomas Piketty, Emmanuel Saez and Gabriel Zucman; the wealth gap of Elizabeth Warren emphasizes on three points. First, under the Warren's wealth tax plan, households would pay an annual 2 percent tax on all assets[63] for net worth equal or less than $50 million and individuals and families who worth more than a $1 billion would pay 3 percent tax.[64] Second, the wealth tax proposal of Senator Warren forecasts a revenue of $2.75

[62] Yglesias, Matthew, "Elizabeth Warren's Proposed Tax On Enormous Fortunes, Explained." *Vox.* (2019). Article. Web.
[63] Farley, Robert, "Facts on Warren's Wealth Tax Plan" *FactCheck.org.* (2019) Article. Web.
[64] Ibid.

trillion[65] that would be allocated in the creation of new government programs such as Universal child care for every child age zero to five; Universal Pre-K for every three and four-year-old; Student loans forgiveness; Free tuition and fees for all public technical schools, two-year colleges and four-year colleges.[66] Third, the Warren wealth tax proposal aims to heavily tax corporations so that they would pay their so-called "fair share."

The Warren wealth tax plan is, in fact, like a form of Robin Hood tax plan in the sense that it seeks to punitively take from those who have access to resources and distribute it to the have-nots. The problem with the Warren's wealth tax plan is that, if this plan is invigorated, it will create three major unintended, yet, detrimental consequences.

---

[65] Ibid.
[66] Ibid.

The first consequence will be the significant expansion of federal authority over the economy. Indeed, Even if in theory the Warren wealth tax plan targets only the super wealthy, this does not mean that the middle-class is exempted from a potential rise in income tax. For Elizabeth Warren to fund all the programs that she wants to implement, taxing the billionaires astronomically won't be enough. The middle-class will be forced to contribute to the funding of these programs, which means that the wealth tax plan of Senator Warren, instead of alleviating the wealth gap, it will reduce the purchasing power of the middle-class, which means that ordinary citizens will have a hard time saving for their retirement or to invest in lucrative ventures. Moreover, the federal government will have extensive power and authority over the allocation of resources and the economy as a whole.

It suggests that the federal government under the wealth tax plan of Senator Warren, will be an omnipotent government that will have absolute knowledge about how to allocate resources and how to invest in these resources. Hitherto, it has been proven countless times that government allocates resources inadequately and inefficiently. For example, government-owned schools underperform compared to charter schools and private schools, and the medical public sector generally delivers low-quality healthcare. If government already delivers such outcomes, what proves that under the wealth tax plan of Senator Warren, resources will be better managed?

The second consequence will be a great decrease in productivity. Indeed, the wealthy are those who have the ability to create capital while the majority of ordinary citizens only have regular jobs that only enable them to pay their bills and feed their families. The wealthy are the ones who have the ability to create jobs. If the wealth tax plan of Senator Warren were to be enforced, the majority of millionaires and billionaires will leave the country. The Warren wealth tax plan may confiscate the material wealth of the wealthy, but it cannot confiscate their knowledge. As knowledge is part of human capital, the wealthy will simply move to a new country and develop the economy of their host. If the wealthy leave the country, the whole pressure of the wealth tax plan will be upon the middle-class, especially on households that make above $100,000. The wealth tax plan of Senator Warren has been already tried in Scandinavian countries, France, Germany, and the United Kingdom. The result was definitely shortcoming. For example, France's wealth tax contributed to the exodus of an estimated

42,000 millionaires between 2000 and 2012.[67] In 1990, twelve countries in Europe had a wealth tax; today, only three countries are using it: Norway, Spain, and Switzerland.[68]

The third consequence is that the wealth tax plan will not directly help those who need it.[69] For the fact of the matter, the expansion of government through the creation of new programs will prevent the poor from being emancipated whether it is economically or psychologically. Too many government programs will disincentivize the most in need to seek higher aims. They will become dependent on those programs, and the government in exchange will seek to control their choices and decisions; like a social contract in which the

---

[67] Rosalsky, Greg, "If a Wealth Tax is Such a Good Idea, Why Did Europe Kill Theirs?" *NPR*. (2019). Article. Web.
[68] Ibid.
[69] Newman, Rick, "3 Problems with Elizabeth Warren's Wealth Tax" *Yahoo Finance*, (2019). Article. Web.

government will provide access for those who lack the means in exchange for the complete obedience from those who need access to these programs. The wealth tax plan of Senator Warren, despite the well-intended programs that it will generate; is merely a tool to aggrandize the power of Washington and to consolidate the centralization of the authority of the federal government.

Essay published on the Mises Institute on October 19, 2019

8

Why The Welfare State Must Be Decentralized Before Being Repealed?

The welfare state, a government-mandated program and institution, was created progressively by the federal government to alleviate poverty and income inequality between individuals and social classes. However, the various programs of the welfare state, have produced a different result; an antagonistic outcome than what was expected. The welfare state was generated in the mid 1930s, following the Great Depression. A set of programs such as Social Security, and the Fair Labor Standard Act, also known as the minimum wage law, were implemented to regulate the economy. These two first and foremost programs enabled the federal government to take control of the economy, and therefore to overstep its authority beyond its initial scope. These two programs alone, transformed the purpose of the federal government from an organization that is intended to protect the rights of the individuals to an arbitrary and punitive institution that would deprive some individuals of their rights in the name of equality. Through the evolution of the twentieth century, the welfare state was substantively enlarged by the successive presidents that used it as a tool to consolidate the power of the federal government. Among the presidents who ruled the United States throughout the last century, President Lyndon B. Johnson was the ruler who significantly aggrandized the welfare state as well as the expansion of the power of the federal government. He passed a series of legislations such as Medicare, Medicaid, the Immigration and Naturalization Act, or the Elementary and Secondary Education Act. These examples of arbitrary legislation effectuated; either by executive order or by congressional approval; to ensure "equality" and "fairness," invigorated two subsequent effects on the American political order.

As a practical matter, the first effect of the welfare is an economic effect. This economic effect created what we know today, as the progressive income taxation. Of course, the progressive income taxation is a form of tax regulation in which the average tax rate increases as the taxable amount increases. The government has been using the progressive income taxation because it enables the application of fiscal policy to retain control over the economy. The substantive goal of fiscal policy is grounded on the use of government spending and taxation to influence the economy when the government controls the prices of goods and services it purchases. The fiscal policy used by the government facilitated the funding of these means-tested programs. Without the progressive income tax, the government would not have been be able to collect enough taxes to subsidize welfare programs. It implies that the government has imposed a compulsory income taxation on those who have earned their money through hard-work and relentless dedication; to assure the transfer of that income or wealth on arbitrarily-created-means-tested programs. Moreover, the subsidization of the welfare state programs did not lift the poorest people; the disenfranchised, and the minority groups; those who did need to be lifted out of poverty. These means-tested programs have been keeping low-income people in a state of poverty by making them dependent on these programs.

Along the economic effects of the welfare state, its policies also had a social effect. The social effect that the welfare state has generated, was the lack of moral individual responsibility. The sad truth is that the liberal policies of the welfare state destroyed some minority communities such as the Black community. The policies of the welfare state did destroy the Black family unit as well as it has emasculated the Black man. The Black man in the family unit, like in any other family regardless of the skin color or culture; represents the authority and the head of the family. In the 1960s, there was only 22 percent of single mothers as head of the household within the Black community. Today, this number has more than tripled. The majority of Black children in low-income neighborhoods grow up without a father in the household because the government instigated higher benefits of means-tested programs to Black women who were not married. These benefits encouraged single Black women to have children out-of-wedlock and to use their welfare benefits as a source of income to live upon. This horrendous practice pushed the Black man to the exit door; to forsake his parental duties as the authoritative figure who would impose discipline and moral compass into the family. The liberal policies of the welfare state also increased the rate of abortion within the Black community. More young black teenagers are having more abortions than any other community in the United States due to a free distribution of birth control pills within the community. The liberal policies of the welfare state destroyed the Black community and impoverished the Hispanic community due to a lack of moral individual responsibility.

The welfare state must be repealed. But to directly repeal it would be aggressive and not wise because there are too many people who currently depend on it. The best way to get rid of the welfare state is to primarily decentralize it. The decentralization of the welfare state would substantially reduce the power of the federal government in the economy and social affairs. Since each state is independent and sovereign from one another, therefore it is up to each state to decide if its government wants to implement a welfare state or not.

The decentralization of the welfare state will force the government to not use a progressive income tax but a flat income taxation. The flat income taxation indicates that the wealthiest individuals will pay a fixed tax. The flat tax means that all people who participate in the productive powers of labor to enhance society's prosperity will all pay the same tax rate. The decentralization of the welfare state will stimulate the individual responsibility of each state. For example, a state like California can afford having a welfare state since its GDP is the strongest among all the states. California can use a progressive income tax to fund these welfare programs, but a state like Kentucky cannot afford having a welfare state because its GDP is considerably low. So, each state can decide, based on its economic growth, if the implementation of a welfare state would help the economy growing or declining.

The decentralization will surely be a step toward a more limited government, a vision that our

Founding Fathers have always praised to ensure liberty and prosperity.

Essay based on lecture at the College of Complexes, June 9, 2019.

9

THE ILLUSION
OF
MEDICARE-FOR-ALL

The idea of having a universal healthcare system
does seem like a moral imperative. Certainly, before
the effectuation of the Affordable Care Act, also
known as Obamacare, millions of Americans were
without health insurance. The moral case for
promulgating universal healthcare is that, it was
said that it is inconceivable to see people dying in
the street because they cannot afford healthcare.
The very purpose of universal healthcare is to

alleviate the cost of medicine by emphasizing on its access.

Medicare-For-All which is properly known as the single-payer system, is the healthcare program that the democratic socialist presidential candidate, Bernie Sanders, has relentlessly avowed in his platform. The single-payer system, in fact, guarantees that all medical care and costs are subsidized by only one payer, which is the government of the United States. If it were to be implemented, the single-payer system would cost $32 trillion for the first ten years of its effectuation according to the Mercatus Center at George Mason University.[70] These $32 trillion will be only generated through heavy taxation to fund the

[70] Reese, Chad, "Medicare for All Would Cost Federal Government $32 Trillion," *The Bridge*, Mercatus Center, George Mason University. (2018). Article. Web.

program.[71] Moreover, as we know that the federal government is the main payer within a single-payer system, it suggests that the government will have the ultimate control over the national healthcare, which means that the government will control the prices and the means of production in the healthcare industry, and it will accordingly determine its supply.[72]

What is the issue with healthcare being subsidized by a central authority? When a central authority subsidizes a program, it means that it also controls the modalities of the program that it subsidizes. The single-payer system will determine who has access to healthcare and under what conditions a patient ought to be seen by a

---

[71] Blahous, Charles, "The Cost of a National Single-Payer Healthcare System," *Mercatus Center George Mason University*. (2018). Article. Web.

[72] Matthews, Merrill, "What Medicare-For-All Supporters Won't Tell You," *Institute for Policy Innovation*. (2019). Article. Web.

government-paid doctor or government-paid nurse. As the sole subsidizer of the program, the government gets to decide of the inventory of the equipment needed to supply medical care; and moreover, the government gets to decide to what extent medical care shall be supplied to patients.[73] When a medical program focuses on access rather than quality; it increases the demands on the one hand because everyone would request that service. There will be more patients everyday requesting various medical care at the same time because they have free access to healthcare and the cost of the service would be relatively low. On the other hand, that augmentation in demand will stimulate a shortage of supply within the service being

---

[73] Greenberg, Jon, "What Is Medicare For All?" Medicare For All: What It Is , What It Isn't?" *Politifact.* (2019). Article. Web.

delivered. As more patients will request medical attention at the same time for various reasons, hospitals will have a hard time supplying different services requested by every patient at the same time. It stipulates that some patients with chronicle conditions may not even be prioritized. They may not be seen by a doctor at their convenience because the increase in demands will generate long waiting lines, and a shortage in staff.[74] That assessment has been proven with the example of the National Health Services (NHS). The National Health Services, which is the nationalized healthcare agency of Great Britain, has already encountered tremendous hardships with the single-payer

---

[74] Conover, Chris, "The # Reason Bernie Sanders' Medicare-for-All Single-Payer Plan Is A Singularly Bad Idea." *Forbes*, (2017). Article. Web.

system.[75] The excess of demand in medical care and the shortage of supply in medical provision and services; forced the British government to hire doctors from India and Pakistan to compensate the shortage of staff that occurred.[76]

Another point that is worth mentioning regarding the problem of the single-payer system is that when healthcare is centralized by the state, it substantially limits incentives for patients and medical staff.[77] Why is that? Healthcare controlled by a central authority attenuates competition and deteriorate the quality of services.[78] If healthcare in the United States was controlled by the federal

---

[75] Barsouk, Adam, "Sanders' 'Medicare-For-All' Won't Work. Here's Why." (2018). Article. Web.

[76] Pipes, Sally, "Why Does the Left Want Universal Health Care? Britain's Is On Its Deathbed." Fortune. (2018). Article. Web.

[77] Dr. Marion Mass, "Medicare for All Will Never Work, So Let's Stop Pushing It." The Hill, (2018). Article. Web.

[78] *Ibid.*

government, competition among hospitals and medical research centers will be surely eradicated because the government will drive these hospitals out of business by monopolizing the healthcare system. If the healthcare system is not controlled by private ownership, and the prices are not determined by the market; the quality of medical services will inevitably and evidently worsen. It will disincentivize doctors to do a better job, it will drive hospitals out of business, and it will create a climate of mistrust between patients and government insurers. Healthcare can always be improved if it is controlled by private insurers who have the power to innovate medicine, and to make arrangements between themselves and patients on premiums. Arrangements cannot be made between patients and government on the cost of medicine. If the single-payer system was implemented here in the United

States, it will be a humongous disaster for our national healthcare system.

10

The Failure Of Socialism:
The Venezuelan Experiment

Socialism has reappeared again as an alternative to capitalism in the United States. In a few words, socialism is a political ideology and an economic system in which the state determines the price of labor, retains the means of productions, confiscate private ownership, and fully controls every aspect of the life of the citizen through coercion in the name of equality. Vladimir Ilych Ulyanov, commonly known as Lenin; was the first political leader on earth to apply the precepts of socialism dictated by Karl Marx; in practice. Subsequently to that, following the Soviet lead, China opted for Socialism with the Cultural Revolution of Mao Tse-Tung; Cuba, Vietnam, most South American, African, and Eastern European countries; have all adopted the socialist model throughout the twentieth century. Interestingly; except for China that was able to switch to capitalism while maintaining an authoritarian system and avoiding an economic stagnation; every other country that have tried socialism as a political regime and as an economic system; has deliberately failed and ended up collapsing. The failure of socialism was epitomized by the dissolution of the Soviet Union in 1991. 1991, marked the ended of socialism as a real political and economic alternative to capitalism, and also marked definitively the prevalence of capitalism as a far better economic system whether we like it or not. The reason why socialism is doomed to be a failed political and economic system is because economically, policies and programs funded by the state are short-term effect; and politically, the state exercises a full and coercive control over society. In other words, socialism is doomed to be a perpetual failure because all aspects (political, economic, and social) of life within civil society are controlled by a central authority. Despite the numerous proofs that substantiated socialism as an unsustainable political and economic system; Venezuela has still fallen for it, and is, today, paying the hard price of its collective mistake.

When Hugo Chavez seized power in the late 1990s and early 2000s, he promised to the Venezuelan people that education, housing, healthcare, access to transportation, and food...that all the basic needs to sustain the human condition will be free to them. That the people of Venezuela would not have to spend a single penny to benefit from these free government-funded programs. Chavez ran for the presidency in 1999 accusing capitalist multinational corporations, private investors, and private businesses to worsen the socioeconomic conditions of the poor. Chavez ran for president on a socialist platform and ensured his people that his administration would make of Venezuela an earthly paradise. From 1999 to 2013, Venezuela was economically thriving, and the people were satisfied with it. How come Venezuela was thriving under a centrally-planned economy? Venezuela has been the first producer of oil in the world. Venezuela is one of the richest countries in the world in terms of raw materials, and oil is the principal resource that supplied the Venezuelan economy.[79] Under the Chavez regime, the economy was prospering because the price of oil was very high. When Chavez began his presidency in 1999, oil prices were $19.35 per barrel to $97.98 per barrel in 2014.[80] The GDP of Venezuela solely rested on oil production.[81] The high price of oil enabled the Chavez administration to fund all these government programs.[82] At the time, the Venezuelan people did not care since they did not have to pay for any of these programs from their own pockets, so they did not care about how these programs were funded. One of the fundamental issues with socialist economic policies is that it incentivizes the ordinary

---

[79] Cowen, Tyler, "Venezuela Isn't Just A Failed State. It's A Failure of the Left." *Bloomberg*. (2019). Article. Web.
[80] Editorials, "Zimbabwe's Coup, Venezuela's Default, And The Ongoing Failure of Socialism" *Investor's Business Daily*. (2017). Article. Web.
[81] Ibid.
[82] Ibid.

citizens to be lazy and more dependent on their government; and it disincentivizes innovation, private and free enterprise to stimulate economic growth. The dependence that Chavez created by funding these government programs, has deteriorated and attenuated the sense of personal and individual responsibility of the Venezuelan citizen. Under Chavez rule, Venezuelan citizens were completely dependent of government's free programs, and on the other hand, Chavez's regime was becoming exponentially and substantially authoritarian. Political opponents were jailed or expelled from the country.

Venezuela's economic problems kicked off exactly in 2015. Chavez died in 2013, Maduro became president in 2014. And the price of oil started to drop. Venezuela's economy is controlled by oil prices per barrel. In 2015, oil prices shrank from $93.17 per barrel to $49.72 per barrel.[83] This significant drop in oil prices created a hyperinflation in goods and services.[84] It has impeded the continuation of these government free-programs. To keep funding these programs, the Venezuelan government had to keep borrowing money. The worst economic decision Maduro has done, was to make the Venezuelan central bank printing more money than it needs while the government is in serious debt. By printing the money that it does not have, the Venezuelan government has generated an economic stagnation; prices of basic goods such as food hygiene idioms have skyrocketed. Today, the Venezuelan economy is collapsing, the political regime has merely become a totalitarian state and Maduro refuses to step down and to free his

---

[83] Rogan, Tom, "Socialism's latest failure: Here's what's going on in Venezuela" *Washington Examiner*, (2019). Article. Web.
[84] Ibid.

people.[85] The political, economic, and social catastrophe that has occurred in Venezuela, is, in fact, another proof that socialism is a failed social experiment that should be never ever tried again.

Essay published on the Libertarian Institute on April 19, 2019

---

[85] Malave, Andres, "How Socialism Failed Venezuela" *U.S. News.* (2016). Article. Web.

11

Capitalism:
The Greatest Economic System To Ever Exist

In today's world; when we speak of capitalism or hear about it; we only hear assertions such as "capitalism is greed", "capitalism creates inequality", "the free-market created the Great Depression"; or "capitalism stimulates more poverty"...and many more nonsensical statements continue to be made against capitalism. Today, capitalism is mostly resented everywhere because it is considered inhumane, immoral, greedy and selfish. Ironically, the majority of people who are resenting capitalism live in capitalistic societies. The very same people who say that capitalism is inhumane are the same who will never dare to live in a country that is not capitalist. They will not dare to move to Communist China, to Cuba, or Venezuela because they very well know that they will not have the freedom they have capitalistic society.

Capitalism is surely not a perfect system. Nonetheless, it is the greatest economic system to ever exist in human recorded history. Capitalism, whether we like it or not, has lifted billions of people out of poverty all around the world. Throughout the twentieth century, communism and socialism were widespread all around the globe. Except for North America, every continent had a socialist/communist state. At the very least. Since the fall of the Berlin Wall, communism and socialism almost disappeared and capitalism has become the main economic system that every society used. Capitalism is a flawed system. Its flaw, however, is a natural and legitimate flaw. Indeed, capitalism is a system of voluntary exchange of goods and services based on a spontaneous order. According to Friedrich von Hayek, capitalism is based on a spontaneous order because it is driven by human action. The concept of human action instigated by Ludwig von Mises, suggests that the exchange of good and services that occurred on a daily basis between people, is made voluntarily and willingly by individuals without any interference from a central authority dictating how the exchange should be operated. Since capitalism is based upon a spontaneous order driven by human action, it entails that the actors of the market must constantly and continuously upgrade their skills in order to meet the demands of the market. The way in which private actors keep up with the demands of the market is through the growth of human capital. So long as human capital continues to germinate, the market continues also to expand because human capital is the essence and engine of innovation and economic stimulation. Therefore, the market can never really fail because if it is about to fail, or if it is failing, there is always a new competitor who brings up a new product on the market at a lower price. For example, despite the economic recession of 2008, new products such the iPhone, WhatsApp, Bitcoin, Spotify, or the iPad; were introduced on the market. These products created a new market venue for private investors. The introduction of a new product or service on the market revamps the economy overall during economic recessions because it creates employment, and subsequently generates a market value for private investors, employers, and employees as well.

Capitalism is the only system that creates wealth. Wealth is generated through employment and employment is incentivized by human capital. Without human capital, there can be no creation of wealth. Socialist countries create more poverty and misery because human capital is undervalued and undermined. Human capital is simply the skills, talents, and abilities that each individual brings into the market. Only capitalism enables human capital to thoroughly demonstrate its full potential. Without a deregulated economy, the free market cannot really thrive because regulations limit the expansion of human capital. If human capital is limited, employment cannot flourish, and no wealth could be created. Socialist economies are doomed to fail because they only rely on a central authority to determine the rules of market. If a central authority is the main actor that determines the rules upon which the economy should be run; through a series of regulations to attenuate competition, then the economy will eventually become stagnant because the central authority lacks the crucial information necessary to develop production. Regulations impede and circumvent businesses to thrive, if businesses cannot thrive, unemployment will skyrocket, and human capital will continue to decline. Regulating human capital is the very first step towards generating poverty and economic stagnation. For example, the implementation of the minimum wage is a regulation of human capital. That is why, increasing the minimum wage to $15 an hour is incentivizing an economic suicide. The more bureaucrats increase the minimum wage, the more they are creating a shortage of human capital, and therefore generating income inequality. Capitalism is thus the economic system which unlocks the potential of human achievement; creates employment as well as wealth and economic prosperity.

12

The Myth Behind The Gold Standard As The Cause Of The Great Depression

Today, the conventional discourse is to believe that the Great Depression was created by a failure of laissez-faire economics; a failure of the free-market; and a failure of an unregulated economy. This is the narrative that has been constructed and which is now construed in all classes of political science and history taught to students. Modern Intellectuals and economists have furthered this narrative by asseverating that the gold standard was the real cause of the market failure, thus government intervention was consequently legitimate to rescue the economy. This is a myth that must be debunked before it indoctrinates the forthcoming generations.

The gold standard did not generate the crash of the stock market of 1929; but the Federal Reserve did. In 1917, the United States was engaged in World War I, and could not subsidize its military expenditures by solely relying on the gold standard. President Woodrow Wilson took the United States economy off the gold standard and used the Federal Reserve to print more money so that the United States government could supply its military arsenal during the war. The early 1920s saw the rise of the Federal Reserve as the central authority which has become the regulator of the value of gold.

Though they thought doing the right thing, the leaders of the Federal Reserve committed the irreparable mistake which unfortunately led to the Great Depression. They passed a law that allowed the Federal Reserve to control the loans and credits that it would offer to commercial banks.[86] This is how the Real Bills Doctrine was implemented.

According to a study conducted by Professor Richard H. Timberlake who has extensively researched on the Real Bills Doctrine and monetary policy; the theory of the Real Bills Doctrine states that the unrestricted issuing of money in exchange for real bills will not cause excessive inflation from undue increase in money supply, and that will not cause bank failure from illiquidity.[87] So, the Federal Reserve supplied an excess of money to commercial banks during times of economic expansion. Based

---

[86] Timberlake, Richard H. "The Original Federal Reserve System" *The Library of Economics and Liberty,* (2016). Article.
[87] Timberlake, Richard H. "Gold Standards and the Real Bills Doctrine in U.S. Monetary Policy." Econ Journal Watch, Volume 2, Number 2, (2005), pp.196-233. Article.

on another study conducted by Professor Lawrence H. White published on Cato Institute, the Real Bills Doctrine wrongly took the nominal quantity demanded of a particular type of credit as a reliable guide to the nominal quantity of money the public wants to hold.[88] Moreover, Professor White argued that the Real Bills Doctrine wrongly made the redeemability of bank liabilities an unimportant aspect in the process that determined the quantity of money. The leaders of the Federal Reserve, in effectuating the Real Bills Doctrine during the 1920s, did not plan in their theory; an alternative response to counter bank panics during times of economic recession. The accumulation of the excess of money supplied to commercial banks by the

---

[88] White, Lawrence H., "Free Banking Theory versus the Real Bills Doctrine", Cato Institute, (2015), Article. Web.

Federal Reserve has generated a substantial deflation. Prices of goods and services significantly shrank below zero percent of the inflation rate; and this deflation subsequently created the crash of the stock market in 1929.

When Franklin Delano Roosevelt became President; one of his major acts as the most powerful man in America, was to increase the value of gold by enacting the Gold Reserve Act.[89] The value of gold increased from $20.67 an ounce to $35 an ounce. Enacted in 1934, The Gold Reserve Act asserted that gold could no longer be retained by private ownership. The law required that gold certificates held by the Federal Reserve through private ownership be surrendered and vested in the Department of Treasury. Only licensed jewelers were allowed to have gold for sales purposes. The

---

[89] "Gold Reserve Act (1934)" *The Living New Deal*. Article.

Gold Reserve Act was the primary policy that, in fact, took the United States off the gold standard before it was utterly dissolved by President Nixon in 1971. The Gold Reserve Act entrenched the nationalization of money and epitomized a clear unjustified encroachment of the central government in the economy. The federal government did not need to take full control of the money-supply to restore the economy. The Federal Reserve could have changed its monetary policy while leaving commercial banks with the power to freely establish their own exchange rates without government interference. Subsequently to this lengthy analysis, it can be confidently conjectured that the gold standard did not create the Great Depression, but the Federal Reserve did.

Essay published on the Foundation for Economic Education and the Libertarian Institute, May 25, 2019

13

The Case for A Flat Income Taxation

There are three main things that no human being can escape. The first is to be born from a woman, the second thing is that we are all going to die one day, and the third thing is we all have to pay taxes until we no longer exist. That being said, whether we like or not, taxes are an important part of our lives. So, it is important to talk about the kind of tax system we have and its effect on our daily lives.

76 percent of the American electorate is in favor of a progressive income tax.[90] Over two-third of the American people believe that the wealthiest members of our society shall pay their "fair share" and 48 percent of the electorate say that taxes are too high in America.[91] Of course, the central issue that motivates people to vouch for the progressive income tax is income inequality. Income inequality between individuals and social classes has given rise to a collective resentment of the middle-class against the top 1 percent. Indeed, politicians on the left say that the top 1 percent owns most of the wealth while not doing much, and the 99 percent, which is basically the rest of the country, owns little while producing most the nation's wealth. For example, the mainstream narrative on income

---

[90] Bach, Natasha, "Most Americans Support Increasing Taxes on the Wealthy" Poll" *Fortune.* (2019). Article. Web.
[91] Ibid.

inequality conveys that CEOs of major corporations earns 300 times more than an average worker.[92]

No one denies that income inequality is not an issue. It surely is. But taxing the rich more than anybody else in order to pay their "fair share" will still not solve the income inequality gap. Many ignore that the top 1 percent is the one that creates jobs and innovates the market economy. Taxing those who have the ability to create jobs and goods and services, does not only penalize production, it also incentives unemployment. A more progressive income tax system may reduce the amount of private savings available to finance domestic investment.[93] This could translate into higher cost of capital and thus impede physical capital

---

[92] "Fact sheet: Taxing Wealthy Americans" *Tax Fairness.* (2014) Data.

[93] Christian E. Weller & Manita Rao, "Can Progressive Taxation Contribute to Economic Development?" *Political Economy Research Institute.* (2008). Study.

formation.[94] For example, states with progressive income tax like Kansas, have seen slower economic growth and faster growth of inequality.[95] In 2017, Illinois, although not being a state with a progressive income tax, had an income tax hike of $5 billion, and this hike mostly affected the middle-class; the social class that was supposed to pay less than the top 1 percent.[96]

The country needs a fairer system, and that system is the flat income tax system. It is fairer than the progressive income tax because everyone pays the same tax rate.[97] Furthermore, the flat tax system encourages economic growth because people would be encouraged to work more so they save more of

---

[94] Ibid.
[95] Oprhe Divounguy, Bryce Hill, Joe Tabor, "Why Illinoisans Should Reject a Progressive Income Tax" *Illinois Policy Institute.* (2019).
[96] Ibid.
[97] Ibid.

their money.[98] For example, let's say Peter and Paul work for the same company but do not have the same salary. Peter is a Junior Associate and makes $60,000 a year and Paul is a Senior Associate and makes $75,000 annually. With a flat income tax system, Peter and Paul will be equally taxed at the same rate regardless of how much each of them makes. If the flat income tax is set at 15 percent for instance, Peter will keep $9,000 after tax-deductible and Paul will keep $11,250 after tax-deductible. This system would incentivize both workers to invest their money in other ventures. Under a progressive income tax system however, Paul would have had less money to save for himself than Peter after tax- deductibles simply because he makes more than Peter. On the moral aspect, the progressive tax

---

[98] Editor-in-Chief, "18 Flat Tax Pros and Cons" *Vittana. Org.* Article.

system is like a punishment system against those who are well-off. It is like punishing them for earning the money they have worked for; like if being rich was a curse. The flat tax system protects all of those who contribute to economic growth. For example, under the proposed flat tax of Senator Ted Cruz, a family of four would not pay taxes on income below $36,000 while those making above that amount will only pay 10 percent on their total income.[99] This system ensures that everyone is able to save as much money as he can. The flat tax system is surely not perfect. Like every system, it has its flaws, but it is a fairer system than the progressive income tax. Under a flat tax system, everyone pays its "fair share" uniformly.

---

[99] Amadeo, Kimberly, "Flat Tax with Its Pros and Cons" *The Balance,* (2019). Article. Web.

About the Author

Germinal G. Van is an author, political essayist, libertarian scholar and philosopher. He is a member of the Libertarian Party of Chicago and a member of the Midwest Political Science Association. He also is an adherent of the Austrian School of Economics. He has published several books and articles with the Libertarian Institute, the Foundation for Economic Education, and Mises Institute.

Originally from Côte d'Ivoire, Mr. Van immigrated to the United States in 2010 with a student visa. He holds a bachelor's degree in political science from the Catholic University of America and a master's degree in political management from the George Washington

University. He is, today, a U.S. Resident. In addition to be a writer and a philosopher, Mr. Van serves as a political advisor to Joshua Flynn, who is a political candidate running for the Illinois State Legislature for District 78 in the 2020 election.

Acknowledgements

The realization of this book came to complete fulfillment thanks primarily to my wife. As usual, she has always supported me in the writing process of each book I have worked on. Her unconditional support remains priceless.

Secondly, I'd like to thank Professor Mohamed Balla Keita. Dr. Keita is an assistant professor of political science at Alabama State University. His intellectual input into this book was a necessary condition to ascertain its completion.

Lastly, I'd like to thank Joshua Flynn who always bring his political insight to the completion of this manuscript.

References

Essay 1: Keynesian Economics is Doomed To Fail

1. Chappellow, Jim, "Keynesian Economics" *Investopedia,* (2019).

2. Worstall, Tim, "If You're A Keynesian Then You Must Believe The Minimum Wage Increases Unemployment" *Forbes,* (2015). Article. Web.

3. Amadeo, Kimberly, "Seven Causes of Unemployment" *The Balance,* (2019). Article. Web.

4. Moore, Stephen, "The Enduring Myth of FDR and the New Deal" *The Heritage Foundation.* (2014). Article. Web.

5. Ibid.

6. Amadeo, Kimberly, "Natural Rate of Unemployment, Its Components, and Recent Trends" *The Balance,* (2019). Article. Web.

7. "Inflation and CPI Consumer Price Index 1940-1949" *Inflation Data.* (2019). Data.

8. Scott Morton, Fiona M. "The Problems of Price Controls" *Cato Institute.* (2001). Article. Web.

9. Ibid.

10. Garrison, Roger, W. "The Absurdity of Keynesian Economics." *Mises Institute.* (2018). Article. Web.

Essay 2: Mixed Economy and the Danger and Central-Planning

1. Arora, Rohit, *Small Businesses Will Be Strangled By a $15 Minimum Wage,* Inc.com. (2017), Article. Web.

2. *Ibid.*

3. *Ibid.*

4. *Ibid.*

5. *Ibid.*

6. Ludwig von Mises, "Ludwig von Mises on the Impossibility of Rational Economic Planning Under Socialism (1922)", *Online Library of Liberty,* Quotation.

7. Allison, Andrew, "The NHS's Flaws Are Killing Us", *Comment Central,* (2018 Article. Web.

8. *Ibid.*

9. *Ibid.*

10. *Ibid.*

11. *Ibid.*

Essay 3: The Three Myth of the Minimum Wage

1. Gardner, Karen, "The Effects of Minimum Wage on Business" *Chron.* (2019). Article. Web.

2. Ibid.

3. Dara Lee Luca and Michael Luca, "Survival of the Fittest: The Impact of the Minimum Wage on Firm Exit" *Harvard Business School.* (2017-2018). Study Data.

4. Ibid.

5. Cost-Benefits Analysis (CBA) *U.S. Small Business Administration.* Data.

6. Ibid.

7. Chabra Esha, "Small Businesses Struggling With $15 Minimum Wage, New Site Reports" *Forbes,* (2017). Article. Web.

8. Ibid.

9. Flynn, Mike, "Minimum wage hikes hurt low-skilled workers" *Employment Policies Institute,* (2006). Article. Web.

10. Ibid.

11. Furchtgott-Roth, Diana, "Column: Raising the Minimum Wage Lowers Employment for Teens

and Low-Skill Workers" *PBS News Hour.* (2016). Article. Web.

12. Ibid.

13. Ibid.

14. Jeffrey Clemens and Matthew Wither, "The Minimum Wage and the Great Recession: Evidence of Effects On the Employment and Income Trajectories of Low-Skilled Workers" *National Bureau of Economic Research.* (2014). Study-Data.

15. Ibid.

16. Ortiz, Alfredo, "Raising the Minimum Wage Will Cut Entry-Level Jobs" *Real Politics,* (2018). Article. Web.

17. Minimum Wage" *Pew Research Center* (2016). Data.

18. DeSilver, Drew, "The Real Value of a $15 minimum wage depends on where you live" *Pew Research Center.* (2018). Article. Web.

19. Ibid.

20. Ibid.

21. "Living Wage Calculator for Waco, Texas." *Living Wage Calculator,* (2019). Data.

22. Living Wage Calculator for District of Columbia," *Living Wage Calculator.* (2019). Data.

Essay 4: The Role of The Government Is Not To Stimulate The Economy But To Let It Regulate Itself

1. Editorials, "Public 2019 Priorities: Economy, Healthcare, Education and Security All Near Top of List," *Pew Research Center,* (2019). Article. Data.

2. Ibid.

3. Ibid.

4. Rosenberg, Jennifer, "32 Ronald Reagan Quotes You Should Know" *ThoughtCo.* (2019). Article. Web.

5. "The Recession of 2007-2009" *Bureau of Labor Statistics.* (2012). Data.

6. Thomas Stratmann and Gabriel Lucjan Okolski, "Does Government Spending Affect Economic Growth?" *Mercatus Center George Mason University.* (2010). Study. Monetary Policy.

7. Ibid.

8. Ibid.

9. Ibid.

10. Ibid.

11. Madzinova, Renata, "The Impact of Government Spending on Income Inequality" *Department of Economics Management and Marketing, College Business, Duchnovičovo,* (2018). Study.

12. Steuerle, Eugene, "Prioritizing Opportunity for All In the Federal Budget" *Urban Institute.* (2016). Article. Web.

13. Steuerle, Eugene, "How Government Tax and Transfer Policy Promotes Wealth Inequality" *Tax Policy Center,* (2019). Article. Study.

14. Analysts, "How Do Taxes Affect Income Inequality?" *Tax Policy Center.* (2019). Data.

15. Ibid.

Essay 6: Big Government Doesn't Make The Economy Better; It Worsens It

1. Helfand, Zach, "The Economist Who Believes The Government Should Just Print More Money" *The New Yorker,* (2019). Article. Web.

2. Youngberg, David, "Bernie's Senior Economic Advisor Sees No Problem in Printing Unlimited Money" *Foundation for Economic Education (FEE).* Article. Web.

3. Sorman, Guy, "Return of The Neo-Keynesians" *City Journal.* (2019). Article. Web.

Essay 7: The Problem With Elizabeth Warren's Wealth Tax Plan

1. Yglesias, Matthew, "Elizabeth Warren's Proposed Tax On Enormous Fortunes, Explained." *Vox.* (2019). Article. Web.

2. Farley, Robert, "Facts on Warren's Wealth Tax Plan" *FactCheck.org.* (2019) Article. Web.

3. Ibid.

4. Ibid.

5. Ibid.

6. Rosalsky, Greg, "If a Wealth Tax is Such a Good Idea, Why Did Europe Kill Theirs?" *NPR.* (2019). Article. Web.

7. Ibid.

8. Newman, Rick, "3 Problems with Elizabeth Warren's Wealth Tax" *Yahoo Finance,* (2019). Article. Web.

Essay 9: The Illusion of Medicare-For-All

1. Reese, Chad, "Medicare for All Would Cost Federal Government $32 Trillion," *The Bridge,* Mercatus Center, George Mason University. (2018). Article. Web.

2. Blahous, Charles, "The Cost of a National Single-Payer Healthcare System," Mercatus Center George Mason University. (2018). Article. Web.

3. Matthews, Merrill, "What Medicare-For-All Supporters Won't Tell You," Institute for Policy Innovation. (2019). Article. Web.

4. Greenberg, Jon, "What Is Medicare For All?" Medicare For All: What It Is, What It Isn't?" Politifact. (2019). Article. Web.

5. Conover, Chris, "The # Reason Bernie Sanders' Medicare-for-All Single-Payer Plan Is A

Singularly Bad Idea." *Forbes*, (2017). Article. Web.

6. Barsouk, Adam, "Sanders' 'Medicare-For-All' Won't Work. Here's Why." (2018). Article. Web.

7. Pipes, Sally, "Why Does the Left Want Universal Health Care? Britain's Is On Its Deathbed." Fortune. (2018). Article. Web.

8. Dr. Marion Mass, "Medicare for All Will Never Work, So Let's Stop Pushing It." The Hill, (2018). Article. Web.

9. *Ibid.*

Essay 10: The Failure of Socialism: The Venezuelan Experiment

1. Cowen, Tyler, "Venezuela Isn't Just A Failed State. It's A Failure of the Left." *Bloomberg.* (2019). Article. Web.

2. Editorials, "Zimbabwe's Coup, Venezuela's Default, And The Ongoing Failure of Socialism" *Investor's Business Daily.* (2017). Article. Web.

3. Ibid.

4. Ibid.

5. Rogan, Tom, "Socialism's latest failure: Here's what's going on in Venezuela" *Washington Examiner,* (2019). Article. Web.

6. Ibid.

7. Malave, Andres, "How Socialism Failed Venezuela" *U.S. News.* (2016). Article. Web.

Essay 12: The Myth Behind The Gold Standard As The Cause of The Great Depression

1. Timberlake, Richard H. "The Original Federal Reserve System" *The Library of Economics and Liberty,* (2016). Article.

2. Timberlake, Richard H. "Gold Standards and the Real Bills Doctrine in U.S. Monetary Policy." Econ Journal Watch, Volume 2, Number 2, (2005), pp.196-233. Article.

3. White, Lawrence H., "Free Banking Theory versus the Real Bills Doctrine", Cato Institute, (2015), Article. Web.

4. "Gold Reserve Act (1934)" *The Living New Deal.* Article.

Essay 13: The Case for a Flat Income Tax

1. Bach, Natasha, "Most Americans Support Increasing Taxes on the Wealthy" Poll" *Fortune.* (2019). Article. Web.

2. Ibid.

3. "Fact sheet: Taxing Wealthy Americans" *Tax Fairness.* (2014) Data.

4. Christian E. Weller & Manita Rao, "Can Progressive Taxation Contribute to Economic

Development?" *Political Economy Research Institute.* (2008). Study.

5. Ibid.

6. Oprhe Divounguy, Bryce Hill, Joe Tabor, "Why Illinoisans Should Reject a Progressive Income Tax" *Illinois Policy Institute.* (2019).

7. Ibid.

8. Ibid.

9. Editor-in-Chief, "18 Flat Tax Pros and Cons" *Vittana. Org.* Article.

10. Amadeo, Kimberly, "Flat Tax with Its Pros and Cons" *The Balance,* (2019). Article. Web.

www.ingramcontent.com/pod-product-compliance
Lightning Source LLC
Chambersburg PA
CBHW020435290526
45785CB00002B/860